Mastering The Mental Side
Of Tournament Golf

Hemispheric
Kinesiology

Ernest Solivan

ISBN: 978-0-6152-1218-0

"Competitive golf is played mainly on a five-and-a-half-inch course...the space between your ears."

Bobby Jones

Table of Contents

Table of Contents

Introduction

It's Sunday morning at the 1996 Masters Championships, and Greg Norman is enjoying a six stroke lead. By the time he signs his score card later that afternoon, he will shoot a 78 and finish in second place behind Nick Faldo for one of the greatest collapses in the history of the Masters.

Professional golfers have a term for this phenomenon and they refer to it as the wheels flying off a player's golf game. They also refer to it as a player's game has gone south, or the player has hit a wall.

Now, Greg Norman is the last tournament player on the face of the earth who needs defending by me or anyone else. Not only does his record speak for itself (91 worldwide wins), but his name will be firmly etched in golf's history books as one its greatest players.

However, we must assume that his goal for that fateful day was to shoot maybe 2 or 3 under, pad his six stroke lead, and not make any costly mistakes. Yet with all his talent and experience he was unable to do it, and there wasn't a thing he could do about. All he could do was helplessly watch his golf game disintegrate before his very eyes.

The focus of this book is to help explain why the wheels flew off Greg Norman's golf game that day and why many of his fellow tournament players both amateur and professional have experienced the same phenomenon during competition. This book will deal with the most neglected and least understood part of the game, the mental side of tournament golf.

Incidentally, Greg Norman is in some pretty good company when you consider that Arnold Palmer, one of the most popular players to ever play the game went into the final round of the 1966 U.S. Open with a three stroke lead. At one point during the round Palmer had increased his lead to seven strokes! On the back nine Palmer's game went south and Billy Casper caught him to tie and eventually win the next day in a playoff.

I will provide you with a tour tested remedy that can be easily integrated into your golf game whether you play in amateur or professional tournaments to help you minimize and/or eliminate those costly mental errors that cause you to mentaly self-destructing during your rounds. This can only be accomplished by understanding the dynamics of your mind and brain, and how they exert absolute control over all physical and mental activity remotely connected to your golf game.

This book does not contain mechanical information such as how to properly hit from a downhill lie, or how to effectively hit out of a bunker. It doesn't matter whether you are staring at a 3 foot putt with a right to left break to make the cut in a particular tournament, or looking at that same putt to win the United States Open.

All the mechanical information you have stored relating to making that putt isn't going to do you a bit of good because it is the activity in your mind and brain that will determine whether you make or miss the putt. Bobby Jones once said the most important part of your golf game is the five inch space between your ears.

Mastering The Mental Side Of Tournament Golf is a book about Hemispheric Kinesiology (HK) and how it can help you maximize that 5 inch space between your ears to help you play your best during tournaments. HK is a success technology that provides you with a perspective that allows you to objectively look at the experiences you are creating on and off the golf course and through that objectivity create positive change that will improve your performance during tournament play and ultimately improve the quality of your life, and isn't that what we are all looking for?

I refer to HK as a language of change because it embodies all the elements necessary to facilitate and accelerate positive change in the players who experience it. HK does not diagnosis or label. Please respect the context in which I present this remarkable and very effective discipline. It works on the simple premise that if it stresses you to play tournament golf, you are not going to do it well. Please set aside your prejudices, beliefs and judgments and do your best to keep an open mind. HK is a little different twist on psychology.

My heart really goes out to professional athletes that play in front of tens of thousands of people. It reminds me of the movie As Good As It Gets. There is a scene where Jack Nicholson is telling Greg Kinnear that he wants to get romantically involved with Helen Hunt. Greg tells Jack, "Go ahead, tell her how you feel about her. The one thing you have going for you is your willingness to humiliate yourself."

The intention of this book is to offer a perspective that may help explain how these past traumatic experiences have created blockages to your success on the golf course, as well as in other areas of our lives. If you already possess the mechanical skills relating to your golf swing, this book will help you accelerate the mental changes necessary so that you may become a complete player.

There is an old saying that you cannot teach an old dog new tricks. This is a testament to how difficult change is for just about everyone. There are basically three elements necessary to create change in your life.

They are Sensation, Perception and Conception. Sensation is the capacity to experience; Perception is the capacity to be aware of what you are experiencing; and Conception is taking action to begin the process of change, or it can also represent a rebirthing into some new experience.

It is said that tournament golf is 95% mental and 5% physical. When you have finished reading *Mastering The Mental Side Of Tournament Golf* you will understand why tournament golf is 100% mental.

The Mind

There is a part of our psyche that has no form, shape or boundaries. It is referred to as the Mind. The Mind is generally thought to be the seat of consciousness. It is made up of every aspect of our being. There are many philosophies that view the Mind in a way that has created numerous fragments, i.e., the spiritual mind, the emotional mind, the etheric mind, etc. I found all these subdivisions of the Mind to be very confusing.

In HK I rely upon the very old axiomatic metaphysical concept known as "cause and effect." Several of the theories that support cause and effect are, "for every action there is an equal and opposite reaction;" "water seeks it own level;" and "what goes around comes around." In Hemispheric Kinesiology, I start by focusing on the desired effect, and work backwards to the cause.

It is important to initially understand that when dealing with the mind, we are dealing with something we cannot see. Although I cannot see a player's Mind, I can see the experiences that player's Mind is creating. For instance, if I am working with a PGA Tour player who has missed 10 cuts in a row, I must assume that he has information stored in his Mind to support him in missing those cuts or he would be doing something else.

Your Mind supports you in everything you do. If you are failing, your Mind is supporting you in failing. It is doing so based upon information it has stored in its memory banks relating to failure and success. The tournament player's physical body is merely acting out (i.e., missing the cut) based upon this mentally stored information, and it is doing it automatically.

To understand cause and effect, you must first understand that before anything physically happens in our lives, it must first start as a thought. The physical body, in turn, reciprocates by creating an experience that responds by corresponding to the thought. When you think negative thoughts, you create negative experiences. When you think positive thoughts, you create positive experiences.

I am very uncomfortable using negative and positive to describe the experiences we all create for ourselves. I prefer to refer to them as desirable experiences versus undesirable experiences. So, if you want to change your undesirable experiences, you must change the thoughts that are responsible for creating those undesirable experiences.

Getting back to the player missing the cut, the information stored in his Mind is the "cause" while the experience he is creating (missing the cut), or the acting out of his physical body is the "effect." The effect, which this player is creating in his reality, is clearly an undesirable effect, and he will continue to create similar experiences until he changes the information responsible for creating them.

The goal of HK is to help change the information in this player's Mind so that he may create a desirable experience (making the cut), and to do it as quickly as possible. Once the information is changed, his experience will change. When you change your thinking, you will change the experiences you are creating with those thoughts. Let's get back to Greg Norman for a minute.

Please don't think I am picking on Greg Norman, but his case is classic and typical of a player who hits a wall during his tournament round. Now, Greg

Norman did not awaken Sunday morning at the 1996 Masters and consciously state, "I think I'll shoot a 78 today and finish in second place." Since that was the experience he created, we have no other choice but to assume that there was information stored in his Mind to support his collapse, or he would have done something else.

It is important to establish a context and foundation whereby all the contributing factors to this sabotaging phenomenon may be examined and understood. The very first thing you must understand is that all we are dealing with when we work with the Mind is information. For instance, although an emotion is something we can feel, it is stored in the Mind as information.

The Mind contains two parts. The Conscious Mind and the Subconscious Mind.

The Conscious Mind

The Conscious Mind is known as the "knower" because it has the ability to be aware of itself. It has the capacity to be aware of what it is thinking and feeling in the normal waking state. It also has the ability to know what it is doing and why.

One of the major functions of the Conscious Mind is that it provides us with volition. Volition is defined in Webster's as, "the act of using the will; exercise of the will as in deciding what to do; a conscious or deliberate decision of a choice thus made."

You are where you are in your life right now as a direct result of the choices you have made using the volitional part of your Conscious Mind. The Conscious Mind provides us with short-term memory and can only focus on one thing at a time. The Conscious Mind uses the five senses; sight, hearing, smell, taste and touch, to collect information which allows it to experience awareness.

The Conscious Mind uses this collected information to formulate your self-image, your prejudices, and your belief system. The most important function of the Conscious Mind is that it allows us to set goals. The information collected by the Conscious Mind will influence the formulation and successful completion of the goals we set throughout our lives.

So, what happens when the Conscious Mind, using its volition, decides to engage in some particular activity like golf? Well, it sends instructions, in the form of a mental memo, to the Subconscious Mind.

The Subconscious Mind

When you engage in an activity, like tournament golf, it is the responsibility of your Conscious Mind to decide the nature of the activity. Your Conscious Mind will send instructions to your Subconscious Mind, "Send me all the information you have relating to playing in a golf tournament."

If the information accessed from your Subconscious Mind is supportive, you will play well in the tournament. However, if the information accessed from your Subconscious Mind is not supportive or contradicts the goal set by your Conscious Mind, you will play badly and probably miss the cut.

Some of the information that may come up for you from your Subconscious Mind that will affect your play that day is, "How many top 10 players are in the field?" "Does the golf course favor right to left ballstrikers?" or "How deep is the rough?" All these elements and many more will influence your play.

The Subconscious Mind is a part of the Mind known as the "doer" because it merely does what it is programmed to do. Unlike the Conscious Mind, the Subconscious Mind does not have the capacity to exercise volition, it merely "does."

The Subconscious Mind acts out through the physical body and uses information it has stored in its memory banks relating to the particular activity. This "acting out" is done instantaneously and automatically. This stored information arrived into the Subconscious Mind through the Conscious Mind using the five senses (sight, hearing, smell, taste, and touch).

The Subconscious Mind is a storage facility for all information that enters through the Conscious

Mind. The one important feature to note about the Subconscious Mind is that when it is storing information it is impersonal. It doesn't say, "I am not going to store this experience because it was a bad experience." IT STORES EVERYTHING!

The Subconscious Mind also provides us with long-term memory, and is where our belief system is housed. Additionally, the Subconscious Mind does not have a sense of humor. Also, the Subconscious Mind cannot distinguish between something real or imagined.

The Subconscious Mind can be likened to the hard drive of your computer with one notable exception. When using a computer, you have the option of saving or erasing the information on your screen. Every piece of information that enters the Subconscious Mind is stored for future use.

Your Conscious Mind will eventually use this subconsciously stored information when it engages in an activity that corresponds to the information in storage. The Subconscious Mind will provide the Conscious Mind with whatever information it has available. The information can be supportive as well as non-supportive in nature.

Some years back, I had worked with a tournament player who played on the mini tours. He confided to me that he had never earned more than $25,000.00 per year playing in tournaments. Using muscle testing, I located the subconsciously stored information causing his problem at age 15. He was able to remember an incident involving a conversation he had with his golf teaching professional. It went something like this:

"My golf teaching professional was telling me that he was quitting golf to sell insurance because he could earn more money selling insurance than playing golf."

Was the information relating to this experience stored in this 15 year old's Subconscious Mind positive or negative? To the impersonal Subconscious Mind it was neither. This teenager learned something about earning money playing golf, and he learned it from someone whom he respected and trusted.

He then stored this information in the memory banks of his Subconscious Mind. Several years later when this player decided to turn professional, his Conscious Mind sent instructions to his Subconscious Mind, "Send me all the information you have stored relating to playing tournament golf professionally."

There was no way this player's Subconscious Mind could support him in earning more than $25,000.00 per year because the information he was accessing from his Subconscious Mind was, "You can earn more money selling insurance than you can playing golf."

Using HK and the techniques outlined in this book, he was able to change that subconsciously stored information. The following year, that player earned more than $80,000.00 playing on the mini tour (Everything is relative). In fact, he qualified for one PGA Tour event that year and made the cut.

If there is one thing I would like you to get from reading this book it's that everything we do is subconscious. Do you remember years ago as a child when you were first learning to tie your shoes? At first it took a tremendous amount of time and effort. Now, you do it without thinking because it has become a subconscious act.

That is exactly what is happening with every other aspect of your life. When you step on that first tee during a tournament you don't have to stop and ask yourself, "What do I do now?" Everything is moving too quickly for your Conscious Mind to get involved and you are at the mercy of the information stored in your Subconscious Mind and it will dramatically influence how you perform that day. That is, your physical body will "act out" based on whatever information is stored in your Subconscious Mind.

There is a very integral component of the Mind that gets involved when the Conscious and the Subconscious Mind interact. It is known as the Critical Factor.

The Critical Factor

After information enters the Conscious Mind, it is reviewed prior to storage in the Subconscious Mind. The responsibility for this task belongs to a component of the Mind known as the Critical Factor. The Critical Factor literally criticizes or reviews information that comes into conscious awareness.

After its review, the Critical Factor must make a decision regarding the disposition of the information. The Critical Factor has two options. It can either store the information, or reject it.

Everyone knows that the color of the sky is blue, but suppose I told you that the color of the sky was red. When that statement enters your Conscious Mind, your Critical Factor will stop it momentarily and says something like, "Let me check the information I have in subconscious storage relating to the color of the sky."

The Critical Factor checks and discovers that the information stored in the Subconscious Mind indicates that the color of the sky is blue. The Critical Factor proceeds to reject the statement, "The sky is red."

Getting back to the player who could not earn more than $25,000.00 per year playing tournament golf professionally, his Critical Factor could not allow him to earn more than that because the information stored in his Subconscious Mind, "You can earn more money selling insurance than playing golf," contradicted the intentions of his Conscious Mind.

Whenever this player got close to earning more than $25,000.00 per year during tournament play, his physical body would create so much stress that his golf swing and golf game would totally fall apart.

It's as if the Critical Factor goes on red alert and using the player's physical body, proceeds to sabotage his golf game.

The Critical Factor isn't being vindictive because it, like the Subconscious Mind, is impersonal. It is merely taking the position that if it cannot find the subconsciously stored information to support the wishes of the Conscious Mind, it is not going to happen. And, the Critical Factor, using every available resource, will do everything in its power to see that it doesn't happen.

This player's physical body could not support him in succeeding because his Subconscious Mind has information stored (earn more money selling insurance then playing professional golf) that contradicts the intentions of the Conscious Mind (to become a successful tour player). It's as if the Critical Factor's hands are tied, and it is saying, "If you want something different to happen, you better change the information stored in your Subconscious Mind."

It is absolutely crucial that you understand the role your Critical Factor plays in sabotaging your tournament play. It is not being vindictive, but rather impersonal. It is basically saying, "I would love to support you in winning a tournament this week, but I just don't have the information stored to support you in doing that." When you change the information, you change the experience.

Imagine the Critical Factor as a guard, and that it is guarding all information coming into and leaving the Mind. How do we change this information? How do we change subconsciously stored information causing us to play way below our potential during tournament play, or causing us to create undesirable experiences in our lives? In order to change subconsciously stored information, we must achieve Critical Factor Bypass.

Critical Factor Bypass

Critical Factor Bypass occurs when new information is allowed to bypass the Critical Factor of the Mind in an effort to change old information stored in the Subconscious Mind. Hemispheric Kinesiology can achieve Critical Factor Bypass, which enables you to literally change subconsciously stored information.

Using HK to achieve Critical Factor Bypass allows us to accelerate change for those who experience it. In order to more fully understand Critical Factor Bypass, we must first look to the advertising industry.

On many occasions advertising agencies will send sales copy to a psychologist, and ask, "Will this copy achieve Critical Factor Bypass for our product?" The ad agencies know that if they can achieve Critical Factor Bypass on anyone who hears or sees their commercials, their chances of selling their product or service are greatly enhanced. They carefully choose the people who star in these commercials, carefully choose the wording, and carefully choose the scenarios.

How can they motivate someone to buy their product or service? One way to do it is using fear. It cannot be done blatantly. It must be subtle. They accomplish this is by using authority figures in their commercials. Have you ever noticed that in many commercials, ad agencies will use policemen, judges, doctors, or firemen?

All these professions represent authority figures and the ad agencies know that when a policeman tells you to do something, you normally do it without question. You do what you are told because the policeman was able to achieve Critical Factor Bypass.

Another very subtle tactic ad agencies will use to create Critical Factor Bypass is race and gender. I once saw a print ad that contained a Caucasian, an African-American, an Asian, an older gentleman, an older woman, a young man, and a young woman. They covered a lot of bases with that ad.

Sometimes the ad agencies will appeal to your emotions. I am certain you have seen the Michelin Tire commercial with a baby sitting in a tire. That commercial has been running for years. This particular commercial has been successful because the ad agency was able to achieve Critical Factor Bypass by using the baby to appeal to the emotions of the viewer.

Babies are harmless, safe and sweet, and just about everyone can relate to babies in a positive way. Michelin must be selling a lot of tires, or they would not continue to use this very effective commercial.

Some of the other tactics used by ad agencies are humor, sex and money. For instance, sometimes the thought of saving money will compel someone to purchase something they don't need. There are many other ways that the ad agencies create Critical Factor Bypass. In fact, the next time you view or hear a commercial advertisement ask yourself, "What are they doing in this commercial to achieve Critical Factor Bypass for their product or service?"

I will explain in a later chapter how we are able to achieve Critical Factor Bypass using Hemispheric Kinesiology. For now, we have examined the nuances of the Mind to include the Conscious Mind, the Subconscious Mind, the Critical Factor, and Critical Factor Bypass. The Mind must act out through the physical body and it does this using the brain.

The Brain

Although the Mind is the decision maker, it is the brain's responsibility to carry out those instructions. The brain is a part of the Central Nervous System composed of approximately 10 billion nerve cells.

Each cell is linked to each other, and together they are responsible for the control of all functions in the physical body from your golf swing to your putting stroke. The brain disseminates these instructions throughout the physical body using information provided by the Mind in the form of electrical impulses.

As I had mentioned earlier, working with the Mind is so challenging because I cannot see it. Although I cannot see a tournament player's Mind, I can ascertain facts by observing what kinds of experiences that player's Mind is creating during tournament play.

The brain is an organ consisting of three major components. The Left Hemisphere, The Right Hemisphere and the Corpus Callosum. Although these three components are integral, they each have very specific and different functions, and can function independently should the need arise.

The Left Hemisphere of the brain controls the right side of the physical body, while the Right Hemisphere controls the left side. (This fact is extremely significant when we begin discussing the golf swing.)

We need only look at a stroke victim to understand this phenomenon. Notice that in the majority of the cases only one side of the body is paralyzed. That's because the hemisphere of the brain on the opposite side of the affected area was so severely damaged during the stroke that it manifested as paralysis.

The affected side of the subject's physical body is not receiving electrical impulses (information) from the damaged hemisphere resulting in partial or total paralysis. There are degrees of physical dysfunction resulting from a stroke, and that total paralysis represents the extreme.

Since the Left and Right Hemispheres of the brain can function independently and have their own responsibilities, they need some way to communicate. This is accomplished using the Corpus Callosum.

The Corpus Callosum is a band of nerve fibers that connect the Left and Right Hemispheres of the brain. The hemispheres share and exchange information (electrical impulses) that will eventually be disseminated to the physical body.

What I realized in my research when I first started working with tour players was that the hemispheres of the brain have a tendency to "weaken" or "switch off." When one hemisphere is switched off, the opposite hemisphere will dominate your activity.

For instance, if a player's Left Hemisphere is switched off, his Right Hemisphere will dominate whatever activity he may be involved in, and vice versa. The hemispheres of the brain are continually influenced by and are reacting to stimuli in a player's immediate external environment.

An excellent case in point occurred when I had worked with the Arizona State University men's golf team in 1991. The director of the golf program was observing one of the sessions with one of the team members on the driving range. He commented that the player was muscle testing weak for everything, as all the statements were relating to golf.

So I turned to the young man and asked him what his favorite college subject was. "Math," he replied. I then asked him to imagine himself doing Math. He muscle tested strong, and both hemispheres of his brain were strong or switched on. Then I asked him to imagine himself playing in a collegiate golf tournament. He muscle tested weak, and both hemispheres of his brain were weak or switched off.

When he was doing Math, his physical body was relaxed, and both hemispheres of his brain were strong or switched on. The information he was accessing from his Subconscious Mind relating to Math supported him in doing it well and he excelled.

However, when he stepped on the golf course, it immediately created stress in his physical body, which weakened or switched off both hemispheres of his brain. Whatever he did on the golf course was a struggle. By the way, this player won his first collegiate golf tournament within thirty days after our session.

The brain does basically three things. It processes (learns), stores, and disseminates information. What kind of information? That would be any and all information relating to pictures, sounds, fragrances, culinary data, and touch.

All three major components of the brain come into play when the brain is exercising these functions. Let's first examine the Left Hemisphere of the brain.

The Left Hemisphere

When the Left Hemisphere of the brain processes (learns) information, it only understands words, language and numbers. That's because the Left Hemisphere processes information sequentially, or one piece at a time.

The Left Hemisphere is one-dimensional, and can only focus on one thing at a time. The Left Hemisphere controls the right side of the physical body and it accomplishes this by sending information in the form of electrical impulses.

When the Left Hemisphere of the brain weakens or switches off, during the processing or learning stage, it's as if a short circuit occurs in the electrical field in the physical body, and the incoming information never reaches the hemisphere of the brain that is switched off. Incoming information will experience difficulty storing in the hemisphere that is switched off.

For instance, if your Right Hemisphere is switched off while your brain is learning, the incoming information will only store in your Left Hemisphere. There was no information stored in your Right Hemisphere because it was switched off. (If the hemisphere is only partially switched off the capacity of the hemisphere to process information is severely diminished.)

When it's time for your brain to disseminate the information to you at some point in the future, you will only receive information from your Left Hemisphere. It's as if you are only getting half the information.

At one seminar I offered for PGA Teaching Professionals, I had a gentleman come up and I asked him to remember learning his golf swing and muscle tested him. The Right Hemisphere of his brain was weak or switched off, while his Left Hemisphere was strong or switched on.

This meant that while he was learning his golf swing, the incoming information only stored in the Left Hemisphere of his brain which caused him to become left-brain dominant relating to what he was learning.

I then gave him a seven iron and asked him to take a practice swing, and muscle tested. The results were the same, Right Hemisphere switched off, Left Hemisphere switched on. Whenever he executed his golf swing, he was left-brain dominant because he was only using information, or using the majority of the information provided by the Left Hemisphere of his brain.

I then asked this PGA Teaching Professional to remember the last golf lesson he had given and muscle tested. The results were exactly the same as the first two, Right Hemisphere switched off, Left Hemisphere switched on. This golf teaching professional was left-brain dominant when he was learning his golf swing, while he was executing his golf swing, and while he was teaching the golf swing!

Every student who learns his golf swing from this teaching professional will become left brain dominant while executing their golf swings. In order to maximize the learning experience, both hemispheres of your brain must be switched on during the learning process.

When the Left Hemisphere of the brain stores information, it will only store sequential information such as words, language and numbers. It will store information that is logical and organized. In other words, the information stored in the Left Hemisphere must be structured.

When the brain disseminates information to the physical body, the Left and Right Hemispheres deal with different and specific information. The Left Hemisphere of the brain provides the physical body with the following information and/or attributes:

Logic, action, decision making, critical, one-dimensional, mechanical, compulsive, doubt, cautious, judgmental, hard working, limitation, shame, rational, stoic, stubborn, organization, reason, pessimistic, specificity, structure, boundaries, rules, rigid, opinionated, intense, impersonal, cold, unfeeling, introverted, controlled, predictable, restricted, precise, serious, conservative, quiet, hard, intolerant, auditory, scientific, temporal (the now), arrogant, and fearful.

When you engage in an activity and the Right Hemisphere of your brain is weak or switched off, your physical body is only receiving information, or a majority of the information, from your Left Hemisphere. This causes you to become left-brain dominant while you are engaged in that particular activity. This causes you to exhibit one or more of the personality traits listed above.

For example, a left-brain dominant individual is judgmental, very critical, and overly structured. This phenomenon can create very dysfunctional experiences for the left-brain dominate individual. Since our thoughts create our experiences, you can clearly see that many of us are only receiving half the information available to us. Where is the other half of this information located? In the Right Hemisphere of the brain.

The Right Hemisphere

When the Right Hemisphere of the brain processes information, it only understands movement and pictures. That's because the Right Hemisphere is spatial and can process information collectively rather than sequentially. This collectiveness allows it to process large amounts of information at one time. It can only process unstructured information.

For instance, if you were looking at a picture of a landscape with your Left Hemisphere, you would have to look at every piece of the picture individually because the Left Hemisphere processes information sequentially. You cannot see the whole picture if you are only looking at one piece.

The collective capabilities of the Right Hemisphere allows you to see the whole picture, while the Left Hemisphere provides you with the capacity to structure the collective information in the form of discernible images.

When we examine this phenomenon during the learning stage of our development, we can clearly see how the hemispheres of the brain influence how we learn. Let's look at an elementary school student named Melvin who is learning to read.

He is learning to read the sentence, "See Jack jump." If Melvin had the Right Hemisphere of his brain weak or switched off while reading this sentence, his Left Hemisphere would dominate. Now, keeping in mind that the Left Hemisphere processes information sequentially, Melvin's Left Hemisphere will know and understand the words see, Jack, and jump.

However, because Melvin's Right Hemisphere is weak or switched off, Melvin will have difficulty achieving total comprehension. In order for that to occur, Melvin would have to send the information from his Left Hemisphere, via the corpus callosum, to the Right Hemisphere, and request additional information such as a visual of a boy jumping. With both hemispheres of his brain participating in the learning process, Melvin will achieve total comprehension, no matter what he is learning.

When the brain disseminates information to the physical body, the Right and Left Hemispheres deal with different and specific information. The Right Hemisphere of the brain provides the physical body with the following information and/or attributes:

Feelings, emotions, relaxation, beliefs, creativity, flexibility, physical movement, tolerance, visualization, artistic, spatial, self-esteem, forgiveness, funny, lazy, love, no boundaries, unorganized, foolish, unstructured, generalizations, procrastination, compassion, optimistic, passivity, unreasonable, loud, expressive, life of the party, passionate, charming, humility, intuition, uncontrollable, multi-dimensional, imagination, addictions, laid back, open-minded and infinite.

When the Left Hemisphere of your brain is weak or switched off, the Right Hemisphere will dominate your activities, from your decision making to your personality. Since your physical body is only receiving information from the Right Hemisphere of your brain, you will exhibit one or more of the above listed personality traits and attributes.

Think of the many times you have you been very passionate about a particular cause or how about the time you bent your putter in half and tossed it into the lake? It is during these times when the

Right Hemisphere of your brain was dominating your thinking.

The objective in HK is to switch on both hemispheres of your brain in relationship to a thought, statement or action. Having both hemispheres of your brain switched on insures that you will have access to information such as judgment, analysis and structure (Left Hemisphere), as well as creativity, imagination and intuition (Right Hemisphere).

With both hemispheres of your brain providing your physical body with information, you will experience total balance in your golf swing and the decisions you make during your tournament play. A great analogy for explaining hemispheric balance is water.

The Right Hemisphere can be likened to boiling hot water, while the Left Hemisphere is ice-cold water. By themselves their temperatures are very uncomfortable. However, when you mix them together you get a warm comfortable and balanced temperature. When both hemispheres of your brain are switched on during your tournament rounds you enter a mental space that athletes refer to as "The Zone."

Another salient difference between the hemispheres worthy of note is that the Left Hemisphere deals with "old" information, while the Right Hemisphere deals with "new" information.

I once did a session with a player and asked him to make a statement relating to winning the next tournament he had entered. When I checked his hemispheres using muscle testing, his Right

Hemisphere was weak or switched off, while his Left Hemisphere was strong or switched on.

The results from the muscle testing told me he was approaching the goal of winning the tournament with his Left Hemisphere and that he was using old information. In other words, he was thinking "What did I do last week to win a tournament; what did I do last month to win a tournament; etc." Without the creativity provided by the Right Hemisphere of his brain, he will continue to use the old information creating the same result.

This may explain why some people seem to make the same mistakes over and over, or repeat the same behavior patterns throughout their lives in spite of their efforts to change. When you are in your Left Hemisphere, you will continue to use old information even though it didn't work last week or last month.

Without the new information provided by the Right Hemisphere in the form of creativity, it's as if you are walking through a mental revolving door. This new information augments and integrates with the old information allowing you to constructively handle whatever challenges you may encounter at that moment.

There is another excellent analogy to contrast the hemispheres of the brain, and how they handle specific tasks. Let's assume that you have just purchased something that requires assembly. The Left Hemisphere of your brain will approach the task by saying something like, "Where are the instructions to this thing?; I can't put this together without the directions!"

Remember that because the Left Hemisphere is using old information, it is basically saying, "Show me the way some else did it, then I can do it." Conversely, the Right Hemisphere will approach that same task by saying, "Hey, even if we don't have the instructions, let's put it together anyway."

That's because the Right Hemisphere is providing the physical body with new information in the form of creativity, and will figure it out eventually. The Right Hemisphere will risk (no instructions), while the Left Hemisphere will tend to play it safe (must have instructions).

When you can play your round with both hemispheres of your brain strong or switched on, you will achieve a level of performance that most players just dream of. With access to structure, judgment and organization (Left Hemisphere), and creativity, intuition and imagination (Right Hemisphere), every decision you make during your tournament rounds supports you in achieving peak performance.

The intention with HK is to help you clear the mental blockages preventing you from playing your best during tournament play. In HK it is imperative that we know what activity is taking place in the physical body in relationship to a statement, thought or action. This is accomplished using Muscle Testing.

Muscle Testing

There are three vital pieces of information necessary in HK in relationship to the subject matter that muscle testing allows me to obtain in relationship to a statement, thought or action. First, muscle testing allows me to determine whether the player's physical body is weak or strong.

Secondly, muscle testing allows me to determine the condition of the hemispheres of the player's brain. Thirdly, muscle testing allows me to post test and validate that the stress has been cleared from the player's physical body.

Muscle testing is a technique that has been widely used in the alternative health field for years and has been used in a variety of applications. I use muscle testing to determine whether stress is present in a player's physical body relating to a statement, thought or action.

Since the physical body is merely acting out based upon information contained in your Subconscious Mind, muscle testing allows me to tap into that subconsciously stored information.

In his book "Switching On," Dr. Paul Dennison defines muscle testing as:

> *"Muscle testing is the art of isolating and testing one muscle at a time in order to determine if it is 'weak' or 'strong', relative to the strength of the individual being tested."*

There are forty-two muscle groups in the physical body. In Hemispheric Kinesiology, I muscle test the deltoid muscle. The deltoid is the larger triangular muscle of the shoulder, which raises the arm away from the side. If you held your right arm straight out from your side, parallel to the ground, and lifted your arm upward from that point, it is the deltoid muscle that allows you to execute that movement.

When I muscle test a player I will ask him to

1.   Stand with weight evenly distributed on both feet;
2.   Hold his left or right arm straight out or parallel to the ground;
3.   I face the player standing in front of the outstretched arm;
4.   I ask the player to look straight ahead and extend the fingers of his outstretched arm so that they are parallel to the ground;
5.   I place my left hand on the player's left shoulder for support;
6.   I place my right hand, using only two fingers (index and middle fingers) on top of the player's outstretched arm between the elbow and wrist;
7.   The player is now ready to be muscle tested;
8.   I will then ask the player to resist upwards slightly, towards the sky, while I apply about 2 ounces of pressure downward towards the ground. This allows both the player and I to get a feel for the muscle test.

The key to muscle testing effectively is 2-2-2. Use two fingers, apply two ounces of pressure, and hold for two seconds. There are two possible responses to a muscle test. Strong, or weak.

A strong muscle test indicates that my downward pressing motion was unable to budge the player's arm. A strong muscle test also indicates that there was no stress present in the player's physical body

49

relating the statement, thought or action for which I muscle tested.

A weak muscle test indicates that the player was unable to resist my downward pressure, and could not hold his arm parallel to the ground. A weak muscle test is evidence that stress was present in the player's physical body relating to the statement, thought or action for which we muscle tested.

What does a strong vs. a weak muscle test tell me, if anything? Well, if I had a player make the statement, "My goal is to win XYZ Tournament," the strong muscle test signifies that the player's physical body would totally support him in winning the tournament because there was no stress present in his physical body relating to the statement.

The absence of stress in the player's physical body indicates that there is information stored in his Subconscious Mind that would support him in winning the tournament. On the other hand, had the player muscle tested weak to the statement, the weak muscle test indicates the presence of stress in his physical body relating to the statement.

It basically stressed the player to say, "My goal is to win XYZ Tournament." The weak muscle test tells me that the information stored in the player's Subconscious Mind would not support him in winning the tournament.

A weak muscle test is the physical body's way of saying, "I am not doing that because I do not have information stored in my memory banks to support you, or that the information I have stored contradicts whatever it is you want to do."

The second piece of information I can obtain using muscle testing is the condition of the Right and Left Hemispheres of the player's brain in relationship to a statement, thought or action.

For instance, when checking the condition of the Left Hemisphere, I merely touch the left side of the player's head and muscle test. If I record a strong muscle test the hemisphere is switched on.

If I record a weak muscle test, the Left Hemisphere is switched off. I would do likewise to check the condition of the Right Hemisphere. Checking the hemispheres of the brain allows me to determine how the player would function while engaged in the activity for which we are muscle testing.

Thirdly, and most importantly, muscle testing allows me to validate, through post testing, that the stress relating to the subject matter has been cleared from the player's physical body. If I have you say "I am the #1 player in the world," and you muscle test weak, and then have you say it again, and you muscle test strong, something obviously changed in your physical body and the way it reacted to the statement.

The problems you are having with your tournament play are not conscious but subconscious in nature. If they were conscious you would be able to correct them consciously. When I say subconscious I mean that it is happening below your level of conscious awareness. You are not aware that you are doing it.

In HK, muscle testing allows me access to a player's Subconscious Mind. If subconsciously stored information is to be changed, it must be done subconsciously.

Muscle testing allows me to inferentially (indirectly) access information from the player's Subconscious Mind using his physical body. That's because the Mind and the physical body are integral and mirror each other. What affects the Mind equally affects the physical body.

When the physical body is in a weakened state, it is engaged in a phenomenon known as "sabotage." Muscle testing allows me to interpret the language used by the physical body to communicate this sabotage state, and that language is Stress.

Stress

WHENEVER THERE IS CONFLICT BETWEEN THE CONSCIOUS MIND AND THE SUBCONCIOUS MIND, THAT CONFLICT WILL ALWAYS MANIFEST IN THE PHYSICAL BODY AS STRESS!

It's as if the Conscious Mind and the Subconscious Mind are not on the same page. When stress is present in the physical body, it will always result in a weak muscle test, and will cause one or both hemispheres of the brain to weaken or switch off. The presence of stress creates a short circuit in the electrical system of the physical body and causes a biological fuse to blow.

It is crucial that you understand this phenomenon because it is at this juncture in the failure process that the physical body begins to sabotage your golf game.

When the physical body is in this stressed state, it goes on red alert because the information in the Conscious Mind does not match the information accessed from the Subconscious Mind. The Subconscious Mind acting out through the physical body will do everything in its power to sabotage your activity.

Taber's Cyclopedic Medical Dictionary defines stress as, *"...the result produced when a structure, system or organism is acted upon by forces that disrupt equilibrium or produce strain...the term denotes the physical and psychological forces that are experienced by individuals."*

Stress has an absolutely pervasive effect on the physical body, and the prolonged presence of stress in the body can manifest pathologically (disease). When stress is present in the physical body, it creates a myriad of physiological changes.

Some of the more salient physical reactions to stress are:
- Increase in the rate and force of heart beat;
- A rise in systolic blood pressure;
- Sweating of the palms and hands;
- Dilation of the pupils;
- Decreased digestion;
- Blood distribution from less to more active organs;
- Increased blood glucose (hyperglycemia);
- Etc;

When stress is present in the physical body, it interrupts the electrical signals between the brain and muscles causing the body to weaken. It is when the body is in this weakened state that the sabotaging phenomenon occurs. You may hit your driver out of bounds, or you may hit a wedge fat and wind up in a water hazard.

This sabotaging phenomenon is so subtle that you will be totally unaware that you are doing it because it is all happening subjectively or subconsciously. That is to say that it is happening below your level of conscious awareness.

All athletic movement, including the golf swing, is subconscious in nature. A golf swing takes a matter of seconds to execute. Remember that earlier we stated that one of the limitations imposed upon the Conscious Mind is that it can only focus on one thing at a time.

The golf swing is occurring too quickly for the Conscious Mind to become involved. Therefore, the physical body is relying totally on the information contained in the Subconscious Mind in order to properly execute the movement.

It is important to note that there are different levels and degrees of stress that may manifest in the physical body ranging from very subtle to very severe. When a tour player executes his golf swing it is impossible to see stress in his body with the naked eye.

However, since his Subconscious Mind stored that information, I can access that information later by merely asking him to remember the golf swing at the moment of impact and muscle test. If he muscle tests weak, then it stressed him to execute his golf swing. If he muscle tests strong, then it did not stress him.

A tour player once asked me why he was able to shoot a 64 during the tournament pro-am and two days later using the same equipment, playing on the same golf course shoot a 74. My reply was that it is not what you are doing, but where you are doing it. Here's why.

Take a 12" wide plank and connect it to two buildings 5 feet off the ground and ask someone to walk across it. No problem. Now, take that same 12" wide plank up to the 30th floor and ask that same person to walk across it. I guarantee you will get a different response. It is not what you are doing, but where you are doing it.

What causes stress to manifest in the physical body besides walking on a 12" wide plank 30 stories high? Well, there is something that occurs while the Subconscious Mind is storing information, and it is responsible for causing stress in the physical body. This phenomenon creates what I refer to as Synthesizing Events.

Synthesizing Events

A "synthesizing event" is created when the emotions from a traumatic experience actually synthesizes (comes together) with the information as it is being stored in the Subconscious Mind.

This synthesized information remains stored and dormant in the Subconscious Mind until the Conscious Mind engages in some activity relative to the information. When the Conscious Mind accesses this synthesized information, it will manifest in the physical body as stress.

One of the best analogies I have heard in describing synthesizing events is to imagine that you have just purchased a brand new boat. The hull of this boat is clean and spotless. As time passes barnacles will attach themselves to the hull. The more barnacles that attach to the hull, the slower the boat will travel, until the boat accumulates so many barnacles it stops all together.

Synthesizing events are like barnacles that have attached themselves to the hulls of our lives. If you accumulate enough barnacles they may manifest physically as a nervous breakdown or chronic illness, and mentally as sabotaging everything you do.

The barnacle analogy is likened to mental baggage that players carry around with them from round to round, and from tournament to tournament. When you accumulate too much mental baggage, the bottom falls out. What's responsible for creating these synthesizing events? Trauma.

Webster's defines trauma as, "1. A bodily injury or shock; 2. An emotional shock, often having lasting psychic effects." Trauma can be experienced both physically and mentally, and can range from mild to severe. The physical trauma from an automobile accident, for example, will heal with time. However, the mental (emotional) trauma may stay in the physical body for years to come unless you take some action to clear and release it.

The intention of Hemispheric Kinesiology is to help players release synthesizing events from their Subconscious Minds manifesting as stress in their bodies. If you have ever missed a three footer to make the cut, or win a tournament, you were traumatized.

There are two types of synthesizing events. The "initial synthesizing event" and the "subsequent synthesizing event." The following analogy explains. Suppose you had a fear of heights. There was a first time you experienced that fear and it is referred to as the initial synthesizing event because it was the first time the synthesizing dynamics came into play relating to the experience.

That synthesized information is stored in your Subconscious Mind and will remain dormant until you go near a high place again. Once this happens, the Conscious Mind sends instructions to the Subconscious Mind, "Send me all the information you have stored relating to being near a high place."

The stored information from the first experience comes up, and since an emotion has synthesized with the information it comes up as well. Your first reaction is, "Let's get away from this ledge!" The second experience created a subsequent synthesizing event.

Once you have left harm's way and are in a safe place, the initial synthesizing event is once again stored in your Subconscious Mind, and the subsequent synthesizing event is stored for the first time. Now you have two subconsciously stored pieces of information (or experiences) to support your fear of heights, and so on.

I can locate and access the initial synthesizing event relating to any subject using muscle testing because your physical body has stored and remembered every experience you have ever had.

Remember the player who couldn't earn more than $25,000 per year playing tournament golf? When his teaching professional quit golf to sell insurance the disappointment traumatized him at age 15. He not only lost his teacher and mentor, but the fact that if his mentor couldn't make it as a tour player, how was he supposed to do it. This trauma stored in his subconscious mind as a synthesizing event.

Some years later when the player eventually turned professional his Conscious Mind sent instructions to his Subconscious Mind, "Send me all the information you have stored relating to playing golf professionally?" Part of the information he accessed was his teaching professional telling him how difficult it was to earn money playing golf professionally.

Clearing the trauma for this player allowed him to break through this mental blockage that had been plaguing him since he was 15 years old. Imagine an onion. Its center represents your potential to become a premier tournament player. Over the years you have accumulated layers of mental blockages (synthesizing events).

These mental blockages are responsible for creating the problems you are now experiencing with your golf game during tournament play. If you don't get rid of them you will carry them with you from round to round, and from tournament to tournament.

In order to access the center of your onion (your true potential), the layers of mental blockages must be peeled away, and that is exactly what Hemispheric Kinesiology will help you accomplish.

It is my belief that 95% of all synthesizing events are stored in your Subconscious Mind during a period in your childhood development krown as The Egocentric Stage.

The Egocentric Stage

There is a period in your childhood known as the egocentric stage, and it occurs between conception and 7 to 8 years of age. It was during this stage in your development when most of the synthesizing events were stored in your Subconscious Mind.

Webster's defines egocentricity as, "Regarding the self or the individual as the center of all things; Having little or no regard for interests or feelings other than one's own; Self-centered." The egocentric child is so self-centered that the first thought they have when something goes wrong in their lives is, "What did I do wrong?"

If you ask a three-year-old boy if he has a brother, he will answer yes. If you ask that same three-year-old boy if his brother has a brother, he will answer no. That's because the egocentric child cannot objectify his experience, he can only experience.

It's as if he cannot see himself. The reason for this phenomenon is that the egocentric child's Mind does not possess a critical factor. Remember that the critical factor allows your Mind to accept or reject incoming information passing through your Conscious Mind.

Without the capacity to criticize incoming information, the egocentric child's Subconscious Mind stores everything! At age 7 or 8 the child's critical factor starts kicking in. During the child's teen years, it is operating at full capacity because teenagers know everything and adults know nothing.

After the teen years our criticalness starts reversing and by middle age most of us experience a softening of our attitudes and come to realize that criticism was all a waste of good energy to begin with.

The absence of the critical factor also denies the egocentric child the capacity to rationalize. You cannot rationalize with someone who is incapable of objectifying his experiences. Some of the other anomalies associated with the egocentric child:

* Absolutize – You either love me or you hate me;
* Personalize - Takes everything personally;
* Idealize their role models – If dad says I'm stupid, it must be true;
* Self-blame – What did I do wrong;
* Shame – There must be something wrong with me;

Children have very limited resources when dealing with trauma. The only way they know how to deal with trauma is to block it out. They accomplish this by switching off one or both hemispheres of their brains depending on the severity of the trauma. This switching off anomaly will influence their behavior and personality for the rest of their lives.

In the 1980's John Bradshaw brought to light a lot of information relating to dysfunctional families. In a dysfunctional family, the members are simply not getting their needs met. But, what kind of a family environment would produce a functional child or adult? The following quote is from a book titled Trauma and Recovery by Dr. Judith Herman:

"The developing child's positive sense of self depends upon a caretaker's benign use of power. When a parent, who is so much more powerful than a child, nevertheless shows some regard for that child's individuality and dignity, that child feels

valued and respected; he develops self-esteem. He also develops autonomy, that is, a sense of his own separateness within a relationship. He learns to control and regulate his own bodily functions and to form and express his own point of view."

Wouldn't it have been nice to have been raised in this environment? The truth is that 99% of all families are dysfunctional. This dysfunction leaves most children who experience it filled with shame and doubt. Dr. Herman continues:

"Shame is a response to helplessness, the violation of bodily integrity, and the indignity suffered in the eyes of another person. Doubt reflects the inability to maintain one's own separate point of view while remaining in connection with others. In the aftermath of traumatic events, survivors doubt both others and themselves."

The switching off anomaly doesn't make children who experience it functional, it makes them more functional. That's because everything is relative. Also, it is during this stage in our development that we accepted beliefs about ourselves that simply were not true. We accepted beliefs that we were not tall enough, thin enough, smart enough, this enough or that enough.

Here is an extraordinary example of how things we learn about ourselves during the egocentric stage of our development stay with us the rest of our lives. One day a teacher asked her students to list the names of the other students in the room on two sheets of paper, leaving a space between each name. Then she told them to think of the nicest thing they could say about each of their classmates and write it down. It took the remainder of the class period to finish their assignment, and as the students left the room, each one handed in the papers.

That Saturday, the teacher wrote down the name of each student on a separate sheet of paper, and listed what everyone else had said about that individual. On Monday she gave each student his or her list. Before long, the entire class was smiling. 'Really?' she heard whispered. "I never knew that I meant anything to anyone!" and, "I didn't know others liked me so much," were most of the comments.

No one ever mentioned those papers in class again. She never knew if the students discussed them after class or with their parents, but it didn't matter. The exercise had accomplished its purpose. The students were happy with themselves and one another. That group of students moved on.

Several years later, one of the students was killed in Viet Nam and his teacher attended the funeral of that special student. She had never seen a serviceman in a military coffin before. He looked so handsome, so mature. The church was packed with his friends. One by one those who loved him took a last walk by the coffin. The teacher was the last one to bless the coffin.

As she stood there, one of the soldiers who acted as pallbearer came up to her. "Were you Mark's math teacher?" he asked. She nodded, "Yes." Then he said, "Mark talked about you a lot." After the funeral, most of Mark's former classmates went together to a luncheon. Mark's mother and father were there, obviously waiting to speak with his teacher. "We want to show you something," his father said, taking a wallet out of his pocket. "They found this on Mark when he was killed. We thought you might recognize it."

Opening the billfold, he carefully removed two worn pieces of notebook paper that had obviously been taped, folded and refolded many times. The teacher knew without looking that the papers were the ones on which she had listed all the good things each of Mark's classmates had said about him. 'Thank you so much for doing that," Mark's mother said, "'As you can see, Mark treasured it."

All of Mark's former classmates started to gather around. Charlie smiled rather sheepishly and said, "I still have my list. It's in the top drawer of my desk at home." Chuck's wife said, "Chuck asked me to put his in our wedding album." "I have mine too," Marilyn said, "It's in my diary." Then Vicki, another classmate, reached into her pocketbook, took out her wallet and showed her worn and frazzled list to the group. "I carry this with me at all times," Vicki said and without batting an eyelash, she continued, "I think we all saved our lists."

If you tell a 6 year old he isn't good enough, he has no way of stopping that information. It goes right into subconscious storage and will be used at some point in his future to create his self-image. If you treat that same 6 years with respect and tell him he is loved and cherished he will, likewise, store the information subconsciously and it will have a profound positive impact on his self-image, and he will carry it with him for the rest of his life.

Many children start learning golf during the egocentric stage of their development. For instance, Arch Watkins started working with Billy Mayfair at age 5. Billy was too small to swing a golf club. So, he worked on putting and chipping which is why Billy always had such a great short game. If you are a coach or teaching professional, please be ever mindful of what to tell these children whenever you interact with them. Because they respect you, the will believe everything you tell them.

If a child is shown respect, he learns to respect himself and others. Disrespecting a child traumatizes him. Sometimes the trauma is so severe that it causes both hemispheres of the brain to weaken or switch off. This creates a condition known as Dissociation.

Dissociation

As I had mentioned previously, children do not have a lot of options when dealing with trauma. Children deal with it by blocking it out. They accomplish this by switching off one of both hemispheres of their brains depending upon the severity of the trauma. When both hemispheres of the brain switch off it creates a condition known as "dissociation."

Dissociation occurs when specific mental functions become separated (or dissociated) from the mainstream of consciousness and, as a consequence, are lost to the individual's awareness and voluntary control.

When a player, for instance, dissociates during a tournament while executing his golf swing, he cannot feel (Right Hemisphere switched off), nor is there structure to his golf swing or mental processes (Left Hemisphere switched off).

Some years back I had worked with an LPGA player before the final leg of the Q School. When I muscle tested the hemispheres of her brain for finishing low enough to secure her tour card both hemispheres of her brain were weak or switched off. She had dissociated. Her physical body had absolutely no idea how to accomplish this goal because there was no information coming from either the right or left hemispheres of her brain.

I decided to do three back to back sessions with this player where I would work her through her bag on the driving range; give her a pre-shot routine; and send her out to play a round of golf. We would meet the following morning on the driving range to discuss her round and do another session if necessary. Her goal or target score was to shoot even par.

74

I met her the next morning on the driving range and asked her what she shot. 12 over par! She was quite disheartened, to say the least, but I had to find out where her game was. The only way I could do that was to have her play a round of golf with a target score. When I asked her what part of her game gave her the most problems she replied, "Everything!"

So I did my best to access and clear as much information as possible about her round and worked her through her bag again. I sent her out for her second round with a target score of even par. We met on the driving range the next morning. When I asked her what she shot she replied sheepishly, "1 over par."

She was able to knock 11 strokes off her game with two sessions because the information causing her problems was hot and readily accessible. I worked her through her bag a third time and sent her out again with the same target score to make sure the session would stick.

When I saw her the next morning there was a smile on her face. "I shot even par" she said. Upon checking with her a week later, she confided to me that she shot 3 under par at a local golf course. She recorded a top 10 finished on the final leg of the LPGA Q School to secure her tour card and went on to win one tournament that year.

If you have ever accepted a belief about yourself that you weren't good enough IT WASN'T TRUE! Please know you accepted that belief during a time in your development when you did not possess a Critical Factor and you were incapable of objectifying and rejecting that information or belief.

There is a way to help athletes keep both hemispheres of their brains switched on during competition and it involves achieving Critical Factor Bypass. This is accomplished with the use of a The HK Performance Trigger.

The HK Performance Trigger

A week before the 1990 Nabisco Tour Championships I worked an HK session with Billy Mayfair at the Camelback Country Club in Scottsdale, Arizona. One of the things I gave Billy to take with him to the Champions Golf Course in Houston, Texas was the HK Performance Trigger. I showed him how to use it in his pre-shot routine.

Playing against the top 30 players in the world, Billy shot 11 under par for the tournament and finished in second place. He went on to finish 12th on the money list that year. For the remainder of this book I will teach you how to use the same trigger to help you play your best during your tournament rounds. You will also learn how to mentally prepare for your tournaments so that you maximize your chances to win.

We now know that when a player experiences a traumatic encounter during his round, the emotions from that trauma will synthesize with the information stored in his Subconscious Mind. In order to clear the synthesizing event a desynthesis must occur.

In other words the emotions that have synthesized with the information stored in the player's Subconscious Mind must be severed. In order to reverse this phenomenon I employ the HK Performance Trigger to facilitate this reversal process.

The HK Performance Trigger is used to release the trauma and all associated emotions connected to that trauma from a player's Subconscious Mind manifesting as stress in his physical body. In other words, the intention of the HK Performance Trigger is to sever the emotional trauma from the information stored in a player's Subconscious Mind creating the stress in his physical body. It works because "energy follows intention."

The more you do something the better you get at it. So, the more you use the HK Performance Trigger, the stronger and more effective it becomes In HK, trauma, synthesizing events and mental baggage are all synonyms.

The HK Performance Trigger was designed to help you peel away these psychological anomalies responsible for your problems during tournament play. Up to this point I have explained how the hemispheres of your brain have a tendency to weaken or switch off and adversely affect your overall performance during tournament play

Let's closely examine how this anomaly specifically affects and influences your golf swing and the flight of your ball.

The Golf Swing

Earlier I had mentioned that when stress is present in your physical body, it will cause one or both hemispheres of your brain to weaken or switch off. This switching off phenomenon not only adversely affects your thought processes during your round, but your golf swing as well. In fact, it will dramatically influence the flight of your ball in a very specific and predictable way.

Here is a rule of thumb regarding the flight of your golf ball in relationship to the hemispheres of your brain:

WHEN YOU HIT TO THE RIGHT OF YOUR TARGET YOU HAVE WEAKENED OR SWITCHED OFF THE RIGHT HEMISPHERE OF YOUR BRAIN.

WHEN YOU HIT TO THE LEFT OF YOUR TARGET YOU HAVE WEAKENED OR SWITCHED OFF THE LEFT HEMISPHERE OF YOUR BRAIN.

Here's why. The right hemisphere of your brain controls the left side of your physical body. The left hemisphere of your brain controls the right side. When your right hemisphere weakens or switches off during your golf swing, it weakens the left side of your body.

When you strike a golf ball with a weak left side, you are going to push it to the right of your intended target. Conversely, when your left hemisphere weakens or switches off during your golf swing, it weakens the right side of your body. When you strike a golf ball with a weak right side, you are going to pull it to the left of your intended target. The opposite occurs for southpaws.

When you strike a golf ball with both hemispheres of your brain weak or switched off (dissociation) there is no telling which direction your ball will travel.

When you execute a golf swing with both hemispheres of your brain switched on, both sides of your physical body remain strong throughout your golf swing and the plane of your golf swing will remain true and constant.

This allows you to strike your golf ball with a swing that is consistent and repetitive. This switching off phenomenon not only dictates how well or poorly you execute your golf swing, but also dictates how you function mentally during your round.

This switching off also affects you on a mental level because it influences the decisions you make during your round. For instance, when you make a decision only using the left hemisphere of your brain, you will have a tendency to play a conservative shot (going for the center of the green).

When you make that same decision using the right hemisphere of your brain, you will take risks (going for the flag sitting behind a sand trap). Making that same decision with both hemispheres of your brain switched on will cause you to make the decision that best supports you in hitting the appropriate shot.

Of all the strokes you will execute during your tournament rounds the one that has the most influence on your final score is your putting stroke.

84

The Putting Stroke

How many times have you heard a TV commentator say about a player, "He is an excellent ball striker, but has always had problems with the short stick."

The putting stroke is a microcosm of the golf swing. The dynamics regarding the putting stroke are identical to that of the golf swing. A player must strike the golf ball square to the target line, and he must strike the ball on the correct plane to insure that at impact the putter makes contact with the ball on or near a very small sweet spot.

When a player is incapable of doing this consistently, he is said to have a case of the "yips." Bernhard Langer, a player who has struggled with the yips most of his career, was asked to describe what it felt like to have the yips. He replied, "Everything is out of whack. It's like your hands and arms are not part of your body." That is exactly what happens when both hemispheres of your brain switch off (dissociation) during your putting stroke.

In fact, the margin for error for your putter is so minute that if you hit a six foot putt with no break, and the face of your putter is open just 3 degrees, you will miss it to the right or left of the hole by 4 inches! To determine what your hemispheres are doing during your putting stroke, we use the same formula as with the driver and irons.

WHEN YOUR PUTT GOES TO THE RIGHT OF THE HOLE (taking the break into account) YOU HAVE SWITCHED OFF THE RIGHT HEMISPHERE OF YOUR BRAIN.

WHEN YOUR PUTT GOES TO THE LEFT OF THE HOLE YOU HAVE SWITCHED OFF THE LEFT HEMISPHERE.

Just as with the clubs, the hemisphere that is switching off will weaken the opposite side of the player's physical body causing the face of the putter to open or close. In the 1989 Masters Championship Scott Hoch missed a 2 foot putt on the first hole of sudden death against Nick Faldo, allowing Faldo to win it on the next hole.

Applying the principles of HK, it is easy to understand that when Scott Hoch hit that putt he had so much stress in his body that he dissociated and switched off both hemispheres of his brain. It was like Bernard Langer said earlier, "Everything is out of whack. It's like your hands and arms are not part of your body."

Here's what may help explain why Scott Hoch missed that putt. It is so important that you understand this phenomenon that I will repeat what I had said in an earlier chapter. IT IS NOT WHAT YOU ARE DOING, BUT WHERE YOU ARE DOING IT! (Read the 12" plank analogy in the Chapter on Stress again.)

There are two very important pieces of information that the brain and the physical body require in order to correctly execute a putt. Alignment, and distance. It is the left hemisphere of the brain that deals with alignment because the left hemisphere deals with linear information. The right hemisphere deals with information relating to distance because the right hemisphere deals with spatial information.

When putting, most players will either get the distance correct and the alignment incorrect, or the alignment correct and the distance incorrect. When both hemispheres are switched on during the putting stroke the distance and alignment are correct and the ball rolls into the hole.

After working a player through his bag, we head over to the putting green. The first thing I do is throw a ball down about 8 feet from the hole and ask the player to read the putt. I then muscle test to determine what his hemispheres were doing while he was reading the putt. I have never muscle tested a player that had both hemispheres of his brain switched on while reading a putt.

The ramifications are obvious. If his right hemisphere is switched off his brain is not receiving information relating to distance. If his left hemisphere is switched off his brain is not receiving information relating to alignment. During the session on the putting green we will use the HK Performance Trigger to switch on the hemisphere that was switched off.

I did a session once with a tournament player and asked him what the weakest part of his game was. Without blinking an eye he replied, "I am a bad putter." It was clear to see that the information stored in this player's Subconscious Mind relating to his putting was, "I am a bad putter." His physical body had no other choice but to act out based upon that information.

I look him straight in the eye and said, "You are not a bad putter. What is happening for you is that you have accepted a belief that you are a bad putter, and your physical body is acting out on that belief." A belief is merely information, and information can be changed. When you change the belief, you change the experience those beliefs are creating. And that is exactly what we did during the session.

Having both hemispheres of your brain switched on while reading and executing your putt allows you to ascertain necessary information relat ng to alignment and distance. It also allows you to keep both sides of your physical body strong during the stroke which dramatically increases your chances of making the putt.

Many of the top players are going to the long putter because they have lost confidence in the traditional short putter. And, remember that confiderce is a mental trait. In fact, one of the greatest players of our time had accumulated over 60 putters in his garage over the course of his career!

The reason so many players go through putters like a hot knife through soft butter is because they have accumulated too many synthesizing events relating to that particular putter. For example, let's suppose you are Scott Hoch on the 18th green at Augusta National and you miss a two foot putt to win the tournament.

That experience no doubt traumatized him. When he stored that event in his Subconscious Mind he also stored the emotional trauma relating to the event creating a synthesizing event. The next time he pulled out his putter his Conscious M nd sent instructions to his Subconscious Mind, "Serd me all the stored information you have relating to this putter."

Since an emotion had synthesized with the stored information it will surfaced as well creating stress in his physical body. The stress will caused one or both hemispheres of his brain to weaken or switch off. Any future strokes he made using that putter were contaminated with the synthesizing event from missing the two footer to win the Masters.

If you have ever missed an important putt and had an emotional reaction afterwards, you just created and stored a synthesizing event. These synthesizing events will store in layers like an onion. When these synthesizing events become too numerous during your putting stroke they manifest as stress and your physical body becomes overwhelmed with this stress every time you touch that putter. Your putting stroke goes south and it's time to get a new putter. The process repeats itself and at the end of your career you wind up with 60 putters in your garage.

The HK Performance Trigger is designed to help you peel away the layers of synthesizing events you have accumulated over the years contributing to your putting inconsistencies and other problems you experience during tournament play. Let's show you how to program in the HK Performance Trigger.

Programming In The HK
Performance Trigger

There are three steps to programming in the HK Performance Trigger:

Step #1: Read the following statement aloud:

"I, (state your name), now accept and integrate into my mind and body the HK Trigger which is stating, thinking or hearing the word 'relax' and touching the thumb and index fingers of both hands, to immediately and permanently neutralize all information manifesting as stress in every cell, organ and tissue of my physical body, and to 'switch on' the left and right hemispheres of my brain as well as my corpus callosum so that all three components function as one allowing me to always remain in present time, and to activate that part of my mind that supports and allows me to experience and be open to receive more wealth, health, happiness, peace, joy, prosperity, safety and security in my life, and all other attributes I may require to help me experience the lifestyle of my choosing, to help me successfully accomplish all my goals, and to improve the quality of my life relating to every statement, thought and action I experience, layers one through infinity, and I will never interfere with the physical manifestation of all my goals, needs and desires, and every time I activate my HK Trigger it will become ten times more powerful, and to allow the HK Performance Trigger to help me always stay calm, relaxed and focused on my goal to win whatever tournament I may be playing; and to help me play to the best of my ability and to help me always stay in the 'Zone' during my competitive rounds; and to help me clear all mental and physical blockages preventing me from winning the tournament."

Step #2: Say the word "relax" and touch the thumb and index fingers of both hands, then release and open your fingers.

Step #3: Read the statement in Step #1 again. (Remember to read it aloud so that you involve as many of your senses as possible.)

When you have finished reading it again, the HK Performance Trigger, (which is stating or thinking the word "relax" and touching the thumb and index fingers of both hands) is now programmed into your Subconscious Mind.

The HK Performance Trigger is intended to help you stay calm, relaxed and focused during your tournament rounds, and most importantly during your golf swing and putting stroke. When you can remain relaxed during the execution of your golf swing or putting stroke, both hemispheres of your brain will remain switched on. In other words, when you are calm and relaxed your brain functions at maximum capacity.

This helps keep both sides of your body strong allowing the plane of your golf swing or putting stroke to remain constant. This ultimately results in more consistent ball striking and putting during your tournament rounds.

The HK Performance Trigger was designed to help you:

• Instantly, automatically and permanently release all trauma from your mind and body manifesting as stress during your tournament rounds;
• Instantly, automatically and permanently switch on and strengthen both hemispheres of your

brain relating to every statement, thought or action you experience relating to your tournament rounds;
•   To remain calm, relaxed and focused during your tournament rounds;
•   To do your best to win whatever tournament you may be playing;
•   Clear all mental and physical blockages preventing you from winning the tournament.

There is an excellent process we use in HK to extract information from your Subconscious Mind. I call it Subconscious Prioritizing.

Subconscious Prioritizing

I had mentioned earlier that one of the limitations of the Conscious Mind is that it can only focus on one thing at a time. If you are having problems with your tournament play, there is usually more than one thing responsible for those problems.

Subconscious Prioritizing is a journaling process that allows you to bring up those problems, or the negative experiences you had during your round, one at a time in order of their priority. Subconscious Prioritizing entails the use of open-ended statements to access subconsciously stored information manifesting as problems during your competitive rounds.

Here's what you do. Grab a pencil and a blank piece of paper draw a line down the center of the page. At the top of the left side of the page write the word Negative. At the top of the right side of the page write the word Positive.

Using open-ended statements list the negative things that occurred for you during your tournament round on the left side of the page. For instance, let's assume that you have just completed the first round of a tournament, and you shot a 74. Here is how you would document this information.

1.   One of the negative things that happened during my first round was I three putted four times.
2.   The second thing was I kept hitting my driver to the left.
3.   The third thing was I didn't birdie any of the Par 5's;
4.   The fourth thing was etc.

After you have finished documenting all the negative things that occurred for you during your tournament round, go to the top of the right side of the page and document all the positive things that occurred for you.

1.   One of the positive things that occurred for me during my first round was I made 4 par saving putts that were 8 feet or longer;
2.   The second thing was I made par on the Par 5 #3 hole even though I hit into a water hazard;
3.   The third thing was I was hitting my long irons very well;
4.   The fourth thing was etc.

It is important to also focus on the positive things that occurred during your round because if you only focus on the negative that is all you will see. It reminds of an old saying I once read.

"You are never as good as you think you are, but you are never as bad either." Looking at both negative and positive elements of your game just gives you a more balanced perspective or what's really going on for you.

As you can clearly see, the Subconscious Prioritizing exercise allows you to document a tremendous amount of information regarding your tournament round and the problems that came up for you.

Now, let's discuss how the HK Performance Trigger is used to clear the information that surfaced for you during your post round evaluation.

How To Use The HK Performance Trigger

With the onion analogy I explained that the center of the onion represents the type of tournament player you have the potential to become. The subconsciously stored synthesizing events (mental blockages) that you have accumulated over the years are responsible for preventing you from becoming that player.

What's creating problems with your tournament play right now is the fact that you carry this mental baggage with you from round to round and from tournament to tournament. It's as if you are carrying the weight of the world on your shoulders.

An excellent example of this phenomenon can be found in Dickens' novel, A Christmas Carol. In particular, the night Scoorge is visited by his dead partner Morley. Morley walks in the door with all these chains around his body and says, "These are the chains I forged throughout my life and now I must carry them with me into eternity."

When you carry chains of synthesizing events with you every time you play a tournament round your performance will be severely compromised. What's very interesting about the Scrooge analogy is that many times after a session with a player they will tell me that they actually feel lighter. Hmm.

If you are really serious about improving your tournament play, I suggest that you do the Subconscious Prioritizing exercise at the conclusion of each and every tournament round.

What follows is a four step process that will allow you to peel away the layers of synthesizing events from your mental golf onion responsible for creating the problems you are now experiencing with your tournament play. In other words, you are going to peel the onion until you get to the center which represents your true potential to become a premier player on your tour.

Step #1: If you haven't already, go back to the chapter on Programming In The HK Perfcrmance Trigger. Program in the trigger by following Steps 1 through 3 (Once the trigger is programmed in you never have to do it again);

Step #2: Read your Subconscious Prioritizing list starting with the negative things that came up for you during your round, and read them one at a time;

Step #3: After reading the first item on the negative side of your list, hit your trigger. Say or mentally state the word "relax" and touch the thumb and index fingers of both your hands, and open them. Move to the second negative thing and do the same thing until you have gone through the entire negative list;

Step #4: Now, move to the positive list and repeat Step #3 until you have gone through the entire positive list;

The reason this technique is so effective is, suppose the first negative thing that happened during your round was that you were hitting your Driver to the left throughout your round. When you read that statement during the clearing process your Conscious Mind will send instructions to your Subconscious Mind, "Send me all the information you have stored relating to hitting my Driver to the left?"

All the information relating to the statement will surface. If there is a synthesizing event connected to the statement hitting your HK Performance Trigger will allow you to subconsciously neutralize it.

This will peel another layer from your mental golf onion responsible for the problems you encountered with your Driver during your round. My suggestion is to punch holes in the completed forms and keep them in a three ring binder.

Once a month or so, review them and see if you can find any patterns that may be developing in your game that may need correcting. In fact, the question you should be asking yourself after each round is, "What could I have done to knock off one or two strokes from my round?"

If you don't think this is effective, Byron Nelson won 18 tournaments in one year back in the 1940's doing the exact same thing. In fact, during that year he won 11 tournaments in a row! (Man, was he switched on or what?) If it worked for him, it will certainly work for you.

The HK Performance Trigger can also be used during your practice sessions and during your tournament rounds as a Pre-Shot Routine.

The Pre-Shot Routine For Drivers And Irons

You will be using a pre-shot routine for one reason and one reason only, to help you become as calm and relaxed as possible during the execution of your golf swing. When you are calm and relaxed your brain functions at maximum capacity.

When you are relaxed during your golf swing, it allows you to keep both hemispheres of your brain switched on. It also allows you to keeps both sides of your body strong allowing your club to remain on a consistent plane throughout your golf swing.

Here's how it works. After selecting the club you have chosen to hit, and are ready to execute your stroke, do the following:

1.   Stand behind your ball and align your ball with the intended target;
2.   Mentally state your goal for the shot;
3.   Mentally state the word "relax" and touch the thumb and index fingers of both hands, and open them;
4.   Walk up to your ball and set up;
5.   Before starting your take away, mentally state the word "relax" and execute your golf swing.

There are many reasons why this pre-shot routine is so effective. The most important reason is that it allows you to remain calm, relaxed and focused. Imagine that your pre-shot routine is a bubble, and that nothing can penetrate that bubble until you have finished executing your golf swing. If something distracts you before you strike your ball, start over and repeat the procedure!

Another excellent advantage in using this pre-shot routine is a phenomenon known as "compounding." Compounding occurs when the same suggestion is layered upon itself many times. The incessant use of the word relax will eventually condition your body to relax. Your play will become much more consistent, and you may even begin to enjoy the experience.

Here is the pre-shot routine for your putting stroke.

The Pre-Shot Routine For Putting

In order to correctly execute a putt, the brain needs information relating to distance and alignment. There are many players who suffer from the yips besides Bernard Langer. The intention of the trigger is to minimize and/or eliminate the yips phenomenon plaguing so many players. This pre-shot routine and trigger have been extremely effective.

Using this pre-shot routine and trigger will help keep both hemispheres of your brain switched on so that your chances of making that 4 footer with a left to right break to save par are greatly enhanced.

The putting pre-shot routine is as follows:

1. Stand to the right or left of your target line (perpendicular) and read your putt to obtain information relating to distance;
2. Stand behind your ball with the hole in front of your ball and read your putt to obtain information relating to alignment and any breaks that may be occurring in your target line;
3. Mentally state your goal for the putt;
4. Mentally state the word "relax" and touch the thumb and index fingers of both hands, and open them;
5. Assume your putting stance and just prior to your stroke mentally state the word "relax" and pull your putter back and execute the stroke.

Mind Mastery For Golf

I created a program for both tournament and recreational players called Mind Mastery For Golf. It includes the DVD Change Your Thinking, Change Your Life, and a powerful 30 minute CD with two tracks. One track is titled Winning At Tournament Golf for tournament players, while track 2 is titled Improving Your Golf Game for recreational players.

The only difference is that one is playing for money, while the other is playing because of their passion for the game. It is designed and intended to work on a subconscious level.

At the beginning of the CD I have programmed in the same HK Performance Trigger (the word relax) contained in this book. The tracks contain over 100 statements relating to your golf swing, each individual golf club in your bag, putting, winning (tournament track), etc. Each statement is followed by the trigger word "relax."

It is recommended that you listen to the CD before and after each tournament round. The CD is designed to work on a subconscious level because that is where your problems lurk. Listening to the CD before your round helps you to mentally prepare for your round by clearing out the cobwebs.

Listening to the CD after your rounds helps to subconsciously clear any synthesizing events that surfaced for you during your round. The synthesizing events that surface for you during your rounds will manifest in your golf game as you missing a 3 foot birdie putt, or perhaps hitting your driver out of bounds.

If you have been a tournament player for 10 years, you have 10 years of information stored in your Subconscious Mind. Your Subconscious Mind is impersonal when it stores information. It stored all your good shots as well as all your bad shots during every tournament round you have ever played.

This information is stored in layers similar to an onion. Most bad shots are followed by some emotional response which stores in your subconscious mind as a synthesizing event, and when accessed at some point in the future will manifest as stress in your physical body.

When stress is present in your body it will cause one or both hemispheres of your brain to weaken or switch off and that is when you will hit an errant shot. The CD along with the Subconscious Prioritizing exercise is intended to help you accelerate the peeling away of the layers of mental blockages preventing you from playing your best during tournaments.

These blockages you have stored over the course of your golfing life are preventing you from playing your best during your tournament rounds. This will not happen over night because these layers of negative information must be removed in layers because that's the way they were stored.

If you set a goal to shoot a certain score during your round and you were unable to do it, please do your best to remain objective and not take it personally. It simply means that your onion needs additional peeling. Do your best to remain objective.

I recommend that you listen to the CD every day for the first 30 days. After 30 days, listen to the CD one to two hours before you tee off. This will provide you with a pre-round mental preparation regime to put you in a mental space that will allow you to play your best.

Also listen to the CD the evening after your round so that you can clear any synthesizing events that may have surfaced for you during your round. You may also listen to the CD as you are drifting off to sleep; while driving in your car; Etc.

Sometimes it is difficult for you to take 30 minutes out of your day to sit down and listen to the audio. If this is the case, I suggest that you buy a small portable CD player and place it at the headboard of you bed. Turn it on before you drift off to sleep with the volume low.

Although the best results will be achieved from listening to the CD while in your waking conscious state, you will derive substantial benefits from listening to the audio as you drift off to sleep.

Let's discuss the importance of setting goals.

Setting Goals

After Tiger Woods won his first Masters he took a week off and came back and won the next tournament. During his post tournament interview, he was asked why he thought he won the tournament. He looked at the interviewer surprisingly and replied, "Because it was my goal to win it."

I believe what sets Tiger Woods apart from other players on the PGA Tour is that he sets goals to win the tournament. He is the only player I have seen interviewed that will actually come out and say that his goal is to win a particular tournament.

When you set a goal to do something, one of two things will happen. You will either succeed or fail. What determines your success or failure is the information contained in your Mind. This stored information is the information you will use while attempting to accomplish your goal.

If the information in your Mind supports you in successfully completing your goal, the accomplishment of your goal will be easy and almost effortless. However, if the information in your Mind does not support you in successfully accomplishing your goal, the accomplishment of your goal will be very difficult and require a tremendous amount of effort.

How does your physical body know what your mind expects from it if you do not set a goal? Set a goal for each shot, each round and each tournament. Even if your body sabotages your efforts when you set a goal, at least give it the benefit of the doubt. ALWAYS SET A GOAL FOR EACH ROUND AND/OR TOURNAMENT!!!

You are setting a goal for each shot when you use your pre-shot routine. Here's how you set your goal for each tournament/round. The night before the first round, grab a pen and paper and write your goal for the tournament/round. Read your goal aloud the night before each tournament/round.

Example goal for the tournament (Write and read the following):

Step #1: I, (player's name), hereby set my goal to win (insert tournament) by shooting the lowest number in the field for the next four rounds. I will play bogey free golf during my rounds and remain calm, relaxed and focused on my goal to win the tournament. I will shoot whatever score is necessary for me to win the tournament and I will not interfere with the successful accomplishment of this goal. This or something better;

Step #2: Hit your HK Performance Trigger by stating or thinking the word "relax" and touching the thumb and index fingers of both hands, and opening them;

Step #3: Read your goal aloud again.

Example goal for the round (Write and read the following):

Step #1: I, (player's name), hereby set my goal for the first round of (insert tournament) to shoot a bogey free round of (insert desired score) and will remain calm, relaxed and focused on my goal to win the tournament and I will not interfere with the successful accomplishment of this goal. This or something better;

Step #2: Hit your HK Performance Trigger by stating or thinking the word "relax" and touching the thumb and index fingers of both hands, and opening them;

Step #3: Read your goal aloud again.

The reason this is so effective is when you make the statement, "My goal is to win XYZ Tournament," your Conscious Mind will send instructions to your Subconscious Mind, "Send me all the stored information you have relating to winning XYZ Tournament."

If there are any synthesizing events connected to that information when it surfaces your HK Performance Trigger will neutralize it. When you listen to the CD as you are drifting off to sleep, you have done everything in your power to mentally prepare for your next round.

Using you HK Performance Trigger during your pre-shot routine the next day will help you remain as relaxed as possible. And, we know what happens when you remain relaxed during your rounds. You enter that domain known as "The Zone."

I once heard an interview with a PGA Tour player where the announcer asked him what his goals were for the coming year. He said, "I don't set goals because it puts too much pressure on me." I couldn't believe what I was hearing! Of course, setting a goal puts presssure/stress on you because when you set a goal that's when your stucco comes up (synthesizing events).

Someone once said, "You can take any road you like, but if you don't know where you are going, that's where you'll end up." Always set a goal for each shot, round and tournament!

Using Your Imagination On The Practice Tee & Putting Green

Imagination is defined as, "The action or faculty of forming mental images or concepts of what is not actually present to the senses." When you imagine yourself doing something, you are going to subconsciously access the same information as if you were physically doing it.

When you are on the practice tee, imagine yourself playing a particular golf course or tournament, hole by hole. Using imagination in conjunction with the HK Performance Trigger allows you to clear any mental blockages you may have stored relating to that hole, golf course or tournament.

Using your HK Performance Trigger on the driving range will make your practice sessions much more effective and meaningful. I suggest that you pick out a target somewhere off in the distance. This will give you a reference point in relationship to the flight of your ball. Remember to always use your pre-shot routine before you strike a golf ball, even on the practice tee.

Pull out your driver and imagine that you are teeing off at the first hole of the tournament you are now playing. Do your pre-shot routine and execute your shot. After striking the ball pay close attention to the flight of the ball in relationship to your target off in the distance. If you hit to the right of your target, you have switched off the right hemisphere of your brain. If you hit to the left of your target, you have switched off the left hemisphere.

After hitting your driver, ballpark the distance to the green on your first tournament hole and pull the appropriate club from your bag and strike another ball using the same procedure. Chances are that you will hit your shot the same way if you were out there on the first hole.

Remember that your mind cannot distinguish between something real or imagined. One day later when you are standing on number one tee, your Mind will think, "Gee, this looks awfully familiar." Mentally work your way through each hole until you have played every hole.

You can also mentally create pressure situations for yourself and determine whether that particular situation would affect your ball striking. For instance, imagine yourself teeing off on the first hole of a sudden death playoff with the number one player on tour.

If you hit a duck hook, chances are you would have hit a duck hook in that situation. You can clear whatever mentally motivated you to hit the duck hook by merely asking yourself, "Why did I hit a duck hook in that situation?"

After asking the question, hit your HK Performance Trigger by saying or mentally stating the word "relax" and touching the thumb and index fingers of both hands, and opening them. Continue to hit balls while mentally creating this pressure situation until you are satisfied with the way you are striking the ball in relationship to the target you have selected.

This is so very effective because when you ask yourself the question, your Conscious Mind will send instructions to your Subconscious Mind, "Send me all the information you have stored relating to why I hit a duck hook in that situation?" If a synthesizing event is accessed, the intention of the HK Performance Trigger is to neutralize it and allow you to peel yet another layer of mental blockages from your golf onion.

I remember working a PGA Teaching Professional through his bag and telling him about how he can use his imagination to help him mentally prepare for tournaments. To prove it, I asked him if there was any particular tournament or event coming up in his immediate future.

He told me that in a week Jack Nicklaus was coming to town for a tournament and that he was going to play a pro-am round with him. He confided to me that he was nervous about teeing off on the first hole with Jack as one his playing partners.

So, I asked him to imagine that he was on the first tee with Jack and that Jack just teed off and hit a drive straight down the center of the fairway 275 yards. I then told him that it was his turn to hit his drive. He proceeded to hit a duck hook, his jaw dropped. He couldn't believe it.

I simply had him ask himself, "Why did I hit a duck hook in that situation?" and asked him to hit his trigger. I then set up the same scenario and asked him to hit his drive again. I went straight toward his target about 260 yards.

Another reason imagination is so effective is that it is the right hemisphere of your brain that provides you with the capacity to imagine. Using imagination during your visits to the driving range or practice tee will switch on the right hemisphere of your brain. If you can keep your Right Hemisphere switched on during practice, chances are you will keep it switched on during your tournament rounds. Since most golfers are left brain dominant (99% of them) you can clearly see how beneficial imagination would be to your practice regimen.

You can also use your imagination on the putting green just before you tee off for your round. The intention is to create as many pressure situations as you can with your imagination. Drop a ball about 8 feet from the hole and imagine you are on the first green putting for a birdie. If you make the putt go to the second hole and repeat the process.

If you miss the putt ask yourself why you missed that birdie putt and hit your HK Performance Trigger and repeat the shot until you make it. Keep going until you have mentally played all 18 holes.

Imagination is so effective that during the final round of the 1994 U.S Women's Open, Lauri Merten was on the putting green imagining herself putting to win the tournament. Four hours later she was hoisting the trophy as the 1994 United States Women's Open Champion. Imagination is a very powerful and effective tool, and it works. I entreat you to integrate it into your practice regime.

Winning

Before you can understand what it takes to become a winner it is important to look at the etymology of the word win. The word win comes from the Greek word "winnen" which literally means "to struggle or contend." However, when we look at Webster's definition of win, we get a different meaning.

Webster's defines win as, "to gain a victory; be victorious; triumph; to finish in first place in a race, contest, etc." What causes an athlete to win? We now know that there must be information stored in his belief system/Subconscious Mind to support him in winning.

How can you determine what's in an athlete's belief system relating to winning? Simply listen to what he had to say when interviewed by the media. Case in point; I once read an interview with a professional golfer who was asked about winning on the PGA Tour.

He was quoted as saying, "The thing is, it's just so hard to win out here. It's incredibly hard." And this player has won two major championships! Now, knowing what we know about the Subconscious Mind and how it stores information, what kind of information do you think is stored in this tournament player's mind relating to winning?

There is no way this player's mind and body can support him in winning consistently because the information he has stored in his Subconscious Mind relating to winning is, "The thing is, it's just so hard to win out here. It's incredibly hard."

Winning for this player will be "incredibly hard" until he changes his subconsciously stored information relating to winning. When you realized that a belief is nothing more than information, and that it can be changed, it makes the process of change less formidable.

HK and this program will help you literally change your beliefs about winning by changing your subconsciously stored information relating to winning.

Webster's defines belief as, "something believed; opinion, conviction; confidence in the truth or existence of something not immediately susceptible to rigorous proof."

If you don't think a person's beliefs can dramatically influence and dictate his decision making throughout the course of his life, try telling someone who has a fear of heights that he has nothing to be afraid of.

What kinds of beliefs, opinions, or convictions do you have about yourself relating to winning? What kind of information do you have stored in your Subconscious Mind relating to winning? What form of rigorous proof can you give me that you are a winner?

To determine what is in your belief system do the Subconscious Prioritizing exercise using the open ended statement, "One of the beliefs I have about being a winner on tour is; The second belief I have about being a winner on tour is; Etc. After compiling your list, go through the answers one by one and clear them using your HK Performance Trigger. If nothing comes up, simply write nothing came up, and hit your trigger.

If you are a tournament player please indelibly etch this next statement into your Subconscious Mind.

YOU CANNOT BE A CONSISTENT WINNER IF YOU DO NOT SET A GOAL TO WIN! ALWAYS SET YOUR GOAL TO WIN THE TOURNAMENT!

I guarantee that if you set a goal to win your next tournament one of two things will happen. You will either have the worst tournament you have had in 5 years, or you will win the tournament. There are two ways to look at something. Positively or negatively, and you are the one who decides which one you will choose.

The reason why it stresses so many players to set a goal is because that is when your "stuff" comes up. If you set a goal to win a tournament and you don't win it, we have to assume that there was information stored in your Subconscious Mind to support you in not winning because it didn't happen.

Please do your best to remain objective and not take it personally. Do the Subconscious Prioritizing exercise after each round with the negative and positive things that occurred during your tournament rounds. Then listen to the CD before and after each round.

This will help to peel away the layers of mental blockages that came up for you during your individual rounds. However, here is what you do to focus on clearing the mental blockages preventing you from winning.

The night before the first round set your goal to win the tournament. (See the chapter on Setting Goals) Remember to also set a target score for each round. If you want to focus your post round evaluations specifically on winning then the exercise must relate to the problems you encountered during the tournament in general. Here's what you do.

After the tournament most players are running to the airport to catch a flight to the next tournament or home. Flying to your next tournament would be an excellent opportunity for you to co your Subconscious Prioritizing exercise.

As with the post round evaluations we will use open ended statements. Let's say you set a goal to win the Phoenix Open and you didn't. On your flight to the next tournament grab a pen and a note pad and begin writing as follows.

One of the reasons I did not win the Phoenix Open was:

1.   I had difficulty finding the fairway with my driver;
2.   The crowds were very intimidating;
3.   Etc. (Keep writing until you run out of reasons.)

When you have finished go to number 1 and read it and hit your trigger. Go to number 2 and read it and hit your trigger. Continue down your list until you have read and cleared every item.

Remember that when you read the statement, "I had difficulty finding the fairway with my driver," your Conscious Mind will send instructions to your Subconscious Mind, "Send me all the information you have stored relating to why I had difficulty finding the fairway with my driver during the Phoenix Open."

Whatever motivated you to experience problems with finding the fairway with your driver at the

Phoenix Open will surface. Hitting your HK Performance Trigger will allow you to neutralize and peel another layer of mental blockages preventing you from winning.

How long will it take? That depends on how many layers of mental blockages/synthesizing events you have stored over the years contributing to your problem. Or, it depends on how big your golf onion is relating to winning. Please remain objective and remember that we are dealing with a tremendous amount of information.

There is one more point I wanted to stress before I move to the next chapter and it somewhat relates to winning and not winning. Get the word "try" out of your vocabulary immediately and keep it out.

During my sessions with players, I will have them state a goal using the word try and muscle test. They will always, without exception, muscle test weak. The word try actually stresses the body.

That's because your Subconscious Mind does not understand the word try. You either do something or you don't. Whenever you hear someone say they are going to try to do something, don't hold your breath. It is probably not going to happen. That goes for tournament leaders who say during an interview after their round that they are going to try to shoot a low number tomorrow.

Now, when I have that player state the same goal and add "I will do my best to..." they will always muscle test strong. Don't try to win the tournament, do your best to win it.

At the risk of being redundant:

YOU CANNOT BE A CONSISTENT WINNER IF YOU DO NOT SET A GOAL TO WIN! ALWAYS SET YOUR GOAL TO WIN THE TOURNAMENT!

Let's discuss how you deal with the media.

The Media

Tour players are very visible personalities and must, at times, have to deal with the media. It is so very important to understand that your body, through your ears, listens to every word you utter. Once stored in your Subconscious Mind these utterances, both negative and positive, are used at some point in the future. And, these utterances have a dramatic impact on your performances during your tournament rounds.

Open the Sports Section of any Sunday paper and read what the leaders of any of the weekly PGA Tour events have to say about their chances of winning the tournament. Do you think what the leader says to the media has any impact on his performance during the final round? Let's see.

It's the end of the third round of the 1990 Nabisco Championship which was played at the Champions Golf Course in Houston, Texas. Billy Mayfair and Jodie Mudd are tied for the lead at 8 under par. A reporter asks both players what they thought their chances were of winning the tournament. Here's how they responded:

> *"I don't see why I can't win."*
> Billy Mayfair

> *"I have already proven that I can win the big one." (He had won the Player's Championship earlier that year)*
> Jodie Mudd

Jodie Mudd won the tournament on the first hole of sudden death. In an earlier chapter I mentioned that our thoughts dramatically influence the experiences we create. Remember that your Subconscious Mind listens to and records everything you say. And, it will use that information at some point in the future.

To prove that this is not an isolated occurrence, at least on the PGA Tour, let's move ahead to the 1997 AT&T National Pro-Am. Upon completing the third round, David Duval is enjoying a three stroke lead over Mark O'Meara. Once again, read what each player had to say to the media about their chances of winning:

> *"O'Meara is on the board and the way he plays here you'd almost have to say he's the front-runner."*
>
> David Duval

> *"All week long I've kind of had this feeling that things were going my way. I feel like there is a guy up there watching over me on the Monterey Peninsula."*
>
> Mark O'Meara

The following day, David Duval shoots a 71 while Mark O'Meara shoots a 67 to win by one stroke. What do you think David Duval's Subconscious Mind, who had a three stroke lead at the time, thought when it heard his statement? In my opinion, David Duval subconsciously conceded the victory to Mark O'Meara at the conclusion of the third round.

If you are leading a tournament after the third round and a reporter comes up to you and asks what you think your chances are of winning the tournament, here's how I suggest you respond.

"Mr. Reporter, my goal coming into this tournament was to win it, and I will do my best to shoot the lowest score in the field tomorrow and finish 1 or more strokes lower than everybody else."

My feeling is that most players will not come out and say they are going to win a tournament because they do not want to appear pretentious. If they don't win it they are left with egg on their face. There is absolutely nothing wrong with setting a goal to win a tournament. If you convey to the media that you are simply going to do your best, and that is all you can ask of yourself, what is wrong with that?

I even heard a player who was leading the tournament say in an interview after the third round, "I'm going to go out tomorrow and make sure that I don't embarrass myself." Notice he did not say anything about winning the tournament. Use terms like: I am going to do my best; If I play the remaining rounds the way I did today, I'd say my chances of winning the tournament are pretty good; I cannot ask any more of myself then to do my best.

Conclusion

In 1997 I received a letter from a PGA Teaching Professional who lived in New York and had purchased the Mind Mastery For Golf program. Here is what he had to say:

"Too much has happened for it to be a coincidence that things turned around soon after your Mind Mastery For Golf program arrived. The First week brought a 3rd place finish in my PGA Regional Club Professional Championship; followed 2 weeks later by a win in our local two day Pro Am.

Interestingly enough the change was not that obvious in my game which has always been erratic but adequate, but more in the attitude that allowed me to get more out of my game. The most obvious change was in the putting where the fear seemed to disappear. A typical example would be standing over a putt as always, but when fear would try to control my thoughts my response would be, 'You can do this, just relax,' and the voice was gone.

In the past when that would happen, I might respond the same way but the thought would push its way back in and distract me making the result hit or miss. Even worse, if I made the putt I came away more with relief and thinking I got away with something rather than with the confidence of accomplishment. That seems to have changed. I am referring anyone who will use your program and I hope they are following through."

I know it is a hard pill for some players to swallow, but it is absolutely imperative that you accept responsibility for the experiences you create on and off the golf course. I don't suggest it so that you can beat yourself up for all the performance problems you are experiencing during tournament play. I suggest it so you can get to the second stage of the change process which is, "If I am creating this experience what can I do to change it?" A funny thing happens when you asked yourself this question. Things start to change.

A wise man wrote years ago that we can't be Batman to all the Robins in the world. You cannot control what others think or feel about you, but you can control what you think and feel about yourself. And, believe me that will be a full time job.

I don't personally know what you are going to have to do to become a better tournament player, but on some level of your awareness you do. Doing this program faithfully will help you peel away the mental blockages preventing you from accessing that information and becoming a premier tournament player.

To gain the maximum benefit from this program it is important to use the entire program which entails:

- Programming in the HK Performance Trigger;
- Using your HK Performance Trigger along with your imagination on the practice tee;
- Using your pre-shot routine before you execute your golf swing and your putting stroke;
- Faithfully doing your post round evaluations using the Subconscious Prioritizing exercise;
- Listening to the CD before and after each round and after each practice session;
- Receiving a relaxing massage the evening before each tournament round.

I suggested a relaxing massage the night before your round because anything you can do to help you to stay calm and relaxed during your round is going to manifest in your game as lower scores.

In closing, please remember that we are dealing with a tremendous amount of information in your Subconscious Mind relating to your tournament play that has been stored over a period of many years. Please do your best to remain objective while using this program.

I trust that I have given you a perspective that will allow you to more fully understand how the hemispheres of your brain influence your performance during tournament play. And, that I have provided you with a remedy that can accelerate positive changes for you not only in your tournament play, but in your personal your life as well.

It is said that adversity introduces a man to himself. I trust that the next time you encounter adversity during tournament play that you will remain objective enough to understand where it came from and how to remedy it. Golf, like life, is relative, and that among the blind, the one eyed man is King. "Relax"

****

HK products available at: www.hk-relax.com &
amazon.com:

Mind Mastery For Golf
Mind Mastery For Hitting
Mind Mastery For Tennis
Mind Mastery For Soccer
Mind Mastery For Pitching
Mind Mastery For Coaching
Mind Mastery For Basketball
Mind Mastery For Winning
Mind Mastery For Learning
Mind Mastery For Money
Mind Mastery For Selling
Mind Mastery For Weight Loss
Mind Mastery For Peace Of Mind
Change Your Thinking, Change Your Life (DVD)

Other books by Ernest Solivan:

Mastering The Mental Side Of Soccer
Mastering The Mental Side Of Tennis
Mastering The Mental Side Of Hitting
Mastering The Mental Side Of Football
Mastering The Mental Side Of Pitching
Mastering The Mental Side Of Coaching
Mastering The Mental Side Of Winning
Mastering The Mental Side Of Basketball
Mastering The Mental Side Of Putting
Quantum Psychophysics
Pro Se Cites & Authorities

For more information about HK contact:
Performance Consultants International
Website: www.hk-relax.com